Double Your Dollar: Tips and Tricks for Saving Money and Getting Bang for Your Buck

Disclaimer and Terms of Use: Effort has been made to ensure that the information in this book is accurate and complete, however, the author and the publisher do not warrant the accuracy of the information, text and graphics contained within the book due to the rapidly changing nature of science, research, known and unknown facts and Internet. The Author and the publisher do not hold any responsibility for errors, omissions or contrary interpretation of the subject matter herein. This book is presented solely for motivational and informational purposes only.

Table of Contents

Introduction

Have you ever wanted to save money to achieve a goal, but do not know how to begin? This book will show you how to save money, achieve your goals, spend time doing the things that you are passionate about, and live a healthier and happier life in the process. Does this sound too good to be true? I promise that it isn't! I have been following the same steps listed in this book for over five years and enjoy living a life of contentment and satisfaction.

Every day you are bombarded by advertisements, commercials, and subliminal messages to purchase and consume more than we need. Because of this, many Americans are in debt and that stops them from realizing their dreams or living up to their true potential. As a consumer, you don't have to follow this system of spending more than you make! Instead you can break the cycle and use the money that you will save by living with only the bare necessities to save, invest and help you retire early. Even after you retire, you can still find fulfillment by adopting a frugal lifestyle.

In the upcoming chapters, you will learn how to set goals, save money, eat healthy, and how to enjoy the meaningful things in life instead of the superficial ones. I promise that as you apply these tips to your life through action, you will notice all of the benefits that I did years ago. It's never too late to adopt a lifestyle of thrift. It can help you accomplish what you never thought possible, allow you to fuel your dreams and passions and help you connect to people like never before. Are you ready to change your lifestyle for the better? Turn the page and let's begin your life-changing transformation from a spender to a saver!

Chapter 1: How a Frugal life Saves you time & Money

Being frugal doesn't mean that you are a cheapskate but rather that you have priorities that are different from the rest of consumerist society. Most people have to have immediate gratification and by adopting frugal principles, you learn how to delay gratification to achieve larger, more important goals, such as financial freedom. If you want to save for a family trip or retire early, you can learn to invest money so that your income works harder for you. These goals are all possible if you adopt a frugal lifestyle.

So what are the benefits to being frugal? There are many different rewards that you gain when you live a frugal lifestyle including the possibility of improved health, appreciation for the items that you have, financial security, and a sense of accomplishment. About 1% of Americans bike to work and experience the health benefits of daily exercise. People that bike, walk, or take public transportation are also leaner than those who rely only on their personal vehicles for commuting. Not only is frugality good for your pocketbook, but it's also great for your health.

Being frugal also makes you appreciate things more. When you focus not on what you are going to get in the future, but rather what you have right now, you find satisfaction in your situation. Sure, you still plan for the future, but what matters most is being happy in the moment. When you achieve one of your goals by being frugal, you also have a response in the reward system of your brain that helps you to move on to bigger and better life goals through maintaining a frugal lifestyle.

One of the biggest benefits to living a frugal lifestyle is the fact that you are able to pay down your debt, save for your goals and invest money to work hard for you so that you don't have to work as much. If you focus on building wealth by saving and investing now, you'll get on a course of financial freedom sooner, allowing you to build wealth instead of debt. Frugal people delay their gratification and only purchase what they need, so that one day in the future, they can have everything that they want.

As you achieve more of your life goals, thanks to your frugal lifestyle, you really have a sense of accomplishment. Sure, you can put a vacation on your credit card and pay off the debt over a few years and make interest payments if you really want to do that. Imagine how much greater you'll feel when you save your income each paycheck and take a trip with your family thanks to your hard work and without borrowing money. Living a frugal lifestyle allows you to not only stay out of debt, but also makes it so that more of your money is saved and invested to pay you a solid monthly income at a later date.

If you're an employee and you aren't being frugal, you're not only losing money, but you are losing time as well. You put a lot of effort into making money every hour you work, and if you waste that hard-earned money on expensive items that have less-expensive alternatives, then you have to work even more hours to make that money back. By doing a little research about the alternatives, you can save money on automobiles, entertainment, clothing, furniture and much more. The savings that you achieve by being frugal and doing your research is worth it when you consider the amount of time it takes you to be able to afford goods and services.

Chapter 2: What are your Passions and Dreams?

What are your passions and dreams? No matter how large or small your dreams are, you should write them down and associate a dollar value and a date to them. Then determine how much money you have to put toward that goal out of every paycheck in order to achieve your dream within the set timeline. If you continue to focus on what you need to do to accomplish your dreams, then nothing is impossible. Even if you don't think that you can achieve all of your goals within a set timeline, at least you have taken the time to determine what your goals are, which is the first step to achieving them.

Although achieving goals can be difficult, it is possible to do this if you work hard and maintain a frugal lifestyle. Sometimes, in order to achieve your larger life goals, you have to make sacrifices. When you adopt a frugal lifestyle, those life changes not only allow you to accomplish your dreams, but they also promote good health, allow you to retire early, and help you to create wealth through saving and investing your money wisely.

What are the things that you are passionate about? Being frugal allows you to put more time and money toward the things that you love, while focusing less on the things that don't matter to you. The more that you save money and time, the more you can spend on building relationships with friends and family, participating in activities that bring you happiness and fulfilment, and the less you have to spend time doing work that you don't enjoy doing. List all of the things that you would like to do if you had all the time in the world. Then decide to live a frugal life and remind yourself of all the things that you can accomplish if you stick to being frugal.

Do you have a tough time holding on to your money, or are you a natural saver? Being frugal will teach you a lot about yourself and can even be a difficult process, at times. The important thing is to be mindful about the times where you fall into old habits and make sure that you change your ways. Everyone fails at some point in a moment of weakness and makes a purchase that exceeds the monthly budget. It's important that when you make mistakes, you learn from them and make sure that it doesn't happen again the next month.

Share your dreams and passions with the world any chance you get. When you share your reason for being frugal, your friends and family start to help you save money and support your decision to live a frugal lifestyle. It's important to get assistance from your loved ones in accomplishing your dreams. It starts with a strong support system that can help keep you accountable in achieving your goals and inspire you when your dreams seem like they're unobtainable.

Start small and make changes that save you money every month. Once you see how easy it is to save money each month, you'll look for other opportunities where you can save an additional dollar. Focus on eliminating common expenses that don't serve you anymore and only distract you from your true goals and passions. Once you have eliminated any excess, search for the large fixed expenses that can save you money. Some people feel like they have to live in a certain area, drive a certain car, or maintain a certain lifestyle. You'll find that you are happier and more fulfilled when you downsize, save money and aren't living a lifestyle of excessive abundance.

Decide to change your life for the better today. Make a list of your goals and passions and keep them somewhere that you will see them every day. When you're budgeting for the next month or delaying the purchase of a luxury item because it doesn't help you achieve your goals, having a list that you can see will help keep you motivated. It's important that you remind yourself why you're living a frugal lifestyle. Keep the goal list updated and check off all the goals that you accomplish. You will notice that you have achieved more in a short period of time than you thought possible and will be closer to living a life of your dreams and passions.

Chapter 3: Simple ways to save Money each Month

Wondering how to save money each month without it being a difficult process? Saving can be incredibly easy, and depending how you normally interact with money, you may want to be more or less extreme about how you fund your savings account. You have two choices, you can either start saving with your normal bank account or for added protection, you can establish a new bank account just for your goals.

If you're not tempted by large amounts of savings and can handle not dipping into your savings account, you can keep your savings connected to your main debit card. Doing so allows you to access your funds in the event of an emergency, but it is also easier to spend. You'll know exactly how much money you have in your account at the end of the month and will gradually watch your savings account increase after every paycheck.

If you aren't sure if you can trust yourself not to spend your savings, pick out a bank that's difficult to access or create an online bank account. Don't order a debit card so that you don't have access to the money and don't even have the statements sent to your house. You will not know how much money you actually have in savings. This will safeguard your money against temptation and make sure that your money actually goes to your goals instead of to a new outfit or something else that doesn't fuel your dreams and passions.

The easiest way to make sure that you save money each month is to make it an automatic process. If your employer offers direct deposit, apply a portion of your income or a set amount of money to your savings account each paycheck. This is known as paying yourself first and can help you establish an emergency savings fund, build your savings account for a trip, or increase the amount of money that you end up investing at a later date.

If your employer doesn't offer direct deposit, make sure that you always place money into your savings account each paycheck as if it's a bill. Once you have placed money into your account each paycheck, after a few months it will become a habit, and you'll do it automatically. If for some reason you forget to save one paycheck, just make sure that you get back on track the next paycheck and make up for the lost savings. If you do this enough, you'll have money saved in no time at all.

Soon you'll learn ways to increase your income if you don't feel that you have enough money left over after paying your expenses. You'll also learn plenty of ways to reduce the amount of expenses that you have so you can put that money to better use over the long-term.

Chapter 4: Affordable Healthy Meals for the Whole Family

One of the easiest ways to save additional money each month is by making wise choices at the grocery store. You can learn how to shop in a low-cost way that's healthy by buying more plant-based, whole foods and reducing the amount of processed foods that you purchase. Plant-based, whole foods include grains, legumes, nuts and seeds, starchy foods and fruits and vegetables. Not only are they the most affordable foods available, but there is also scientific evidence that eating a diet rich in plant-based, whole foods has significant health benefits and reduces and reverses some of the most common diseases that plague the United States today.

Buy your staples in bulk while they are on sale. Rice, beans, oats and tons of other foods keep for a long time and are the basis of any healthy meal. You can save money each month by purchasing in bulk at wholesale stores. Plan your meals ahead of time so that you know exactly what foods you need and only go to the grocery store when you are running low on food and need to purchase new items.

Keep your meals simple for the greatest health benefits. Have a grain, a green, and legumes with every meal to support a healthy diet. You'll get all of the essential nutrients that your body needs by eating these food groups. Eat a variety of healthy food and you'll not only feel great, but you'll notice changes in your overall health and well-being. People who adopt a plant-based, whole food diet slim to a healthy weight, feel full for a longer period of time, and fight off heart disease, some forms of cancer and many other problems.

With manufactured food, you get a bunch of additives that take out the nutrients of the food and add chemicals that you don't need in your diet. Plus, with every process that food goes through, there are added costs associated to the change. You can make foods that are more delicious than the processed foods in very little time each day. You'll control exactly what is in your food. You'll notice the difference in how you feel each day by just removing all of the processed foods and junk food from your diet.

Start paying attention to the food labels to see exactly what you are putting in your body. If the food label has lots of words that you cannot pronounce, avoid it! If you see lots of salt, fat or oil, find an alternative or better yet, make your own with whole foods. It's surprising to hear that the healthiest foods for you are actually the least expensive foods to buy, but it's the truth! If you really want to save money on your grocery bill, learn more about eating plant-based, whole foods and the health benefits that you and your family will receive by following a diet rich in whole foods.

Chapter 5: Frugality Tricks to Teach Your Children

Frugal families have specific and realistic priorities in life. Your family can adopt a frugal lifestyle by making choices to save money on unnecessary expenses so that you can put more money toward important goals, such as college tuition, retirement and investing. Frugal families enjoy home-prepared meals and stretch out their income by not eating out as frequently. They clip coupons together, focus on buying necessities instead of unnecessary luxuries, make the most of free community events to provide entertainment for the whole family and create lasting memories. They strive to lessen the electric bill by making sure that every light is turned off after leaving the room and that every electronic gadget is unplugged. By practicing such habits, frugal families are able to live a debt-free, peaceful and quality life. The great news is that it's very easy to teach your children and family members how to be frugal and why it's important.

Start by explaining money to your children at an early age. When kids start to understand that you are the one who decides which toys, food and goods are bought at the supermarket, introduce them to the value of cash. Teach your children about paying for goods and services by having them hand money to the checkout person at a grocery store or making them insert coins in vending machines and parking meters to familiarize them with money. Allow them to play age-suitable computer games available on the Internet that teach financial skills to children. One such game is Money Metropolis in which children aged 7 to 12 learn how to earn money by doing chores for people while playing educational games.

It doesn't have to be a challenge to raise frugal kids! Eventually, they'll understand that it's not the money you spend that makes you happy but rather the memories you create with the people you love. When they ask you to purchase something, explain to them the other alternatives that you can put that money toward. Give them an allowance for completing chores and have them save for the items that they want to teach them the value of a dollar. Open a bank account to teach them about saving, withdrawing and investing money. It might pique their curiosity, and they will want to learn more about it. How excited would your children be to add money into their bank account from the hard work they've done? Think about how happy they'll be once they have saved enough money to purchase their favorite toys and even have money left-over for their next purchase. This experience will help your children learn that everything in life costs something and that you have to work hard in order to gain what they want.

Children adopt the habits of their parents, and therefore, the best that you can do to teach your children a frugal lifestyle is to adopt one yourself. Explain the difference between wants and needs with your own purchases and explain to them how you are living within your means instead of borrowing money. This will teach your kids that everything they want isn't necessarily required in order to live a happy life. Children who learn this will grow up into strong and resilient adults and understand why it is important to save, spend wisely and invest money from a young age. They will also learn to be happy without a lavish lifestyle and to appreciate people for who they are and not for what they have. Spending quality time with their family in a park while playing and enjoying nature will give them more solace and peace of mind than playing alone with expensive toys. They will also experience a sense of family bonding. All these benefits can be helpful in raising unmaterialistic and smart children so that they develop into productive and independent adults.

Frugally-raised kids also develop entrepreneurship skills. When children are taught to set goals and save money to acquire them, they are actually learning time-management skills. When a child owns their own bank account, they become financially literate and learn about the concept of investing. Brainstorming about different ways to earn income to save for a goal makes your children more creative and business minded. When a child thinks of saving money to acquire a new toy, he is actually learning how to become dependent on himself for his success. All such acts will infuse entrepreneurship skills in your children and raise them as independent adults who can turn into successful entrepreneurs and economically benefit society.

Teaching your children about being frugal, explaining that they should spend money on the things that they need instead of what they want and giving them important lessons about money management will create lifelong skills that they'll use throughout adulthood. Make learning about frugality a fun activity for the whole family, and they'll begin to see its importance by identifying ways to save money. Once you have the support of your family, all of your saving goals are achievable. Remember to celebrate with your loved ones when all of your hard work pays off!

Chapter 6: Saving Money on the Necessities of Life

It's really important that everyone realizes the importance of saving money to survive not just today but also in case of any financial emergency that may arise. In order to follow a well-organized saving plan, you must thoroughly reconsider and evaluate your income and expenses. The next step is prioritizing your expenses and eliminating what isn't necessary. You should clearly understand the difference between essential and nonessential expenses. There are expenses that you have to pay every month like house rent, the cost of your meals, utility bills and debt payments. There are some expenses that can be avoided or reduced, such as your luxury shopping and entertainment expenses. When you adjust your budget to save small amounts in each spending category, you'll find that the little changes add up to a large amount at the end of the month.

People around the world adopt different lifestyles. Some people adopt a lifestyle of abundance and purchase lots of luxuries like the updated smartphones, luxurious vacation plans, and they attend lavish gatherings. Unfortunately, many people cannot actually afford such a lifestyle and end up going into debt, pushing back their retirement age and failing to invest money to make their income work hard so that they don't have to. Other people adopt a frugal lifestyle, invest intelligently and save money for the things in life that are not categorized as superficial. Making the change from a lifestyle that chases abundance to one that is more frugal has long-term benefits and is easy to adopt. Let's discuss the different ways that you can save money on the necessities of life.

If you want to save money on food, you have to be aware of how you eat. You previously learned that the lowest-priced whole foods are not only the least expensive, but they are the healthiest for your family. Food consumption is a basic necessity and spending your food budget wisely at the grocery store can help you save additional money each month. Restaurant dining costs four times more than meals that are consumed at home. If you enjoy eating at different restaurants, then cut down on the amount of times you dine out by preparing a majority of meals at home. Treat yourself to a restaurant meal during happy hour as a treat for sticking to your budget or just avoid it altogether. Also, food recipes can be cooked in large quantities at once, allowing you to freeze or store smaller portions throughout the week. Use weekly grocery sales and coupons to get food items at lower prices. You'd be surprised how much of your family's income can be saved by creating better eating habits.

Another major expense that you can save money on is your housing cost. This doesn't necessarily mean you have to move to a new city or state. If moving doesn't seem possible, you can stay in the same town and find less-expensive housing options. Take note of your needs and consider moving to an affordable house in a less-expensive area to cut down on rental expenses. If you can find work in a different geographical location, consider moving out of the state you live in right now. If the cost of living is lower, you enjoy the culture, and it has the necessities that you and your family needs, you can save hundreds of dollars each month by leaving an expensive area. Yes, it might seem scary to make a move but chances are if you think back to all of the places that you have traveled, there are at least a few places that you've enjoyed and could imagine living in if the cost is lower than where you currently live.

Purchasing second-hand goods is a great way to save money on the items you need. Replace household items with used counterparts instead of spending on a brand new item. If you have toddlers, you do not need to spend much on their clothing. Children often grow so fast that their sizes change within months. You can often find slightly worn or even brand new children's clothing at second-hand shops.

Purchase items in bulk whenever you can. This goes for food as well as basic, everyday items that you need. There is a significant difference in the cost of buying a single item or a bulk pack of the same item. It's best to purchase the things that you constantly use in bulk while it's on sale, even if you don't think you'll need that many of the item for a few months. Chances are the prices might not be as low in the future, and you'll make significant savings. Also, plan to buy clothes and other items only during sales that are on the off-season. By purchasing things while they are inexpensive, you save lots of money that you can put toward your savings and investing goals.

Save money on communication and entertainment expenses by using an inexpensive cell phone with an affordable plan, looking for alternatives to your current Internet package and by reducing your cable package or canceling your television service altogether. Everything has an alternative and to save money, all you have to do is learn about the various service competitors and opt for the most economical one.

There are some larger expenses that unintentionally become part of our everyday life. These include credit card and loan payments, buying cigarettes and alcohol, unused memberships and other activities. Eliminating such expenses can boost your savings. Although it may be difficult to quit drinking or smoking altogether, a reduction in both activities will save you money and can have benefits to your health.

The budgeting plan that you adopt should be flexible, reasonable and realistic enough to face any circumstances that are part of life. Make changes to your life gradually in a way that's sustainable. Change is a gradual process, so whenever you notice yourself breaking your budget, or wanting to splurge on a purchase, remember that you are reducing your expenses for a purpose and get yourself back on track. Your savings at the end of the month will contribute to a huge, annual savings. Whenever you deviate from your plan, find motivation in that fact that you'll avoid financial stress issues in the future and experience a more content life than those who overspend.

Chapter 7: Helpful tips for low-cost Transportation

Transportation, for most people, is a large expense that takes up a considerable portion of a household budget. Between car payments, gas prices, car maintenance and insurance, it's easy to spend lots of money to get where you need to go. The use of low-cost transportation for everyday travel can help you save money, promote your health and benefit the environment. Depending upon the location of your work and whether you need to take other people to different locations during the day, some forms of transportation might work better for your lifestyle.

When you think about low-cost methods of transportation, you don't normally consider cars. However, it's convenient and fast to use your own personal vehicle to commute, which is what makes it such a popular method of transportation. As a frugal buyer, purchase a reliable car at a good price. Consider the miles per gallon and make sure that you purchase a car with cash instead of relying on an auto loan, which puts you in debt and requires you to pay interest every month.

If driving a car is the only way you can travel, it's helpful to reduce commuting fuel costs. You can do this by searching for a gas station offering the lowest rates on gas in your area. Carpool with other people to save money by sharing the responsibility of paying for gas and for driving. Also make sure that your vehicle is serviced properly. To save on gas, your tires need to be properly inflated, and your oil should be changed regularly. Avoid the use of your car's air conditioning and heating unit to save on fuel. Check if your employer covers a portion of your transportation expenses, especially if you commute a lot for your job.

Now let's discuss the most frugal forms of transportation. Low-cost methods of commuting include walking, riding a bike and using public transportation. Biking is one of the most inexpensive modes of commuting. Buying a bike and keeping it in working order every month can be done at a fraction of the price of the monthly upkeep and costs of a car. Most people live within five miles of where they work and those who bike have the additional health benefits of daily exercise, enjoy a safer form of transportation and save money every time that they commute with their bike.

Similarly, walking to work is a low-cost method of transportation that does not require any commuting costs other than time. Both biking and walking nourish your psychological and mental health. Commuting daily by riding a bike or walking engages you in physical exercise and helps burn calories. The sweat released from exercise activates chemicals that help overcome stress, anxiety and depression. If you had a rough day at the office, a walk or a ride back home can boost your mood. Moreover, people with jobs that require them to sit all day can make the most of walking and biking to stay active and promote physical health and well-being. The health benefits that arise from daily exercise has even been shown to increase job performance!

Riding your bike and walking also help the environment. Since there is no fuel consumption, no vehicle emissions are released into the atmosphere, and you are doing your part to help reduce the environmental footprint. Riding your bike or walking during rush hour can even save you time and money in the long term, while reducing the amount of congestion on the road.

Public transportation is another affordable method of commuting. With public transportation, you don't need to worry about paying for parking or maintaining your vehicle, and your transportation expenses are greatly reduced. You can purchase discounted monthly and annual passes to save lots of money. If you take public transportation for just a few days a week instead of driving, you'll notice lots of savings that you can apply to different goals.

During your commute on public transportation, you can relax, read, listen to music, take a nap, communicate with other passengers and take in the natural scenery, which is something you normally can't do while driving. In regions with extreme weather conditions, it's not always possible to commute on foot or bike, and public transport can be the most convenient and economical mode of traveling.

Just like walking and riding your bike benefits the environment, public transportation also greatly reduces pollution in highly-populated cities. Public transport is cheap and many employers offer free passes, which make public transportation affordable for their employees.

Every individual has a different level of health, and the important thing is to consider your goals while commuting. If you are looking to exercise more, you can rely on many of the frugal methods of transportation like walking and biking. If you want to just save some money every once in a while, consider commuting via public transportation to benefit not only yourself but also the environment.

Chapter 8: Increasing your Income to meet your Goals

It's very common for people who are taking care of their family to need additional income in order to reach any savings goals. Start with your current job and see if you can work an extra shift, get a raise or find a better paying job that's similar to the one you currently have.

Once you have done all that you can to maximize the income from your job, you may want to consider getting a second source of income. A second income helps you achieve your goals even faster, boosts the amount of savings that you have and helps pay off your debts faster. If you are already making frugal choices but have a problem making ends meet or saving money to achieve your goals, it's important that you focus on increasing your income.

When people want to make more money, they immediately think of acquiring a second job. It's important to find a second job that is flexible about the hours your work and allows you to do something that you enjoy. If you aren't passionate about your second job, it can be easy to experience burn out, especially if your family also demands a lot of your time and attention after working. Having a second job can also insure that, in the event that anything happens to your main source of income, you already have a steady paycheck until you find a replacement position.

There are many options to choose from when you decide to work part time. Try to find a second job that pays you well for your extra time and effort. Since you are working additional hours a day, you'll have less time left for your hobbies and interests. Choose a second job based on your passions so that you don't feel overworked and stressed out. If you can't find a job that interests you and pays well, it's probably a good idea to go into business for yourself.

If your full-time job has you up on your feet all day, consider a job that allows you to relax and be creative. Working from home is a great opportunity, and there are many different services and goods that you can do to make extra income, depending on your skills and the things that you are passionate about.

If you possess aesthetic sense and graphic designing skills, you can take graphic designing projects as part-time work. You can utilize your singing skills to earn an extra income by giving lessons and become a teacher. Working as a musician in gigs can help you in fulfilling your passion but can also serve as a source of solace. If you like to write, you can earn a second income writing a blog or working for others. It is a lot of fun to express your ideas and connect with an audience of readers. Plus, if you're successful at it, it will really pay off! Once you have established an informative blog, you can put ad content on the page that's relevant to your blog content and earn passive monthly income. You can even write product reviews on your blog and get paid by the brands in return for sales.

Freelancing has become a reputable and rewarding way to earn extra income online. It allows you to work your own schedule without being bound by long-term contracts. Instead, you can be self-employed and enjoy financial freedom. There are so many opportunities for freelance writers who offer copywriting, copy editing and technical writing services. If you love to take photographs, you can sell your work online. If you like to code or program computers, you can make an income building websites or applications for clients. The opportunities are endless.

If you are an experienced writer, you can make good money by writing ebooks. Publishing platforms like Kindle and Smashwords™ provide numerous opportunities for writers to upload their ebooks. An ebook community of readers is where people can learn about your newest releases, shop, download, and read your ebooks. These platforms offer 35% to 70% royalty rates to the authors, which can be a great source of income. You can write content based on your interests and passions. If you are tech savvy, you can even develop user manuals and guides related to the products that are currently in demand. If you enjoy fiction writing, you have a plethora of topics to choose from like romance, detective cases and crime thrillers. Once you are done writing, upload your ebook with an eye-catching cover and market it on social platforms. You may earn a huge monthly income on Amazon's Kindle platform if your book attracts the right audience.

Chapter 9: Saving, Investing and Planning for Retirement

Many people work to enjoy luxuries, but one of the main goals of someone who is frugal is to save and invest their money so that they can retire early. When you have a frugal lifestyle, you are able to put more money away so that it continues to work for you even after you're finished working yourself. Adopting a frugal lifestyle allows you to set aside a large portion of your income every month and meet your savings and investing goals.

It may be a strange thought to consider retirement in your early twenties when one has many glamorous years of living yet to do. The fact is that it's never too early to start planning for your retirement, and your twenties are the perfect time to consider a financial plan to save and invest money. Investing today allows you to live a financially free and happy tomorrow.

Of all your priorities for following a savings plan, retirement is one of the most important goals that can be easily overlooked. You should be financially stable and independent enough to take care of yourself in your golden years. To ensure that you maintain the same quality and standard of living after retirement as your present status, you need to devise a strong retirement plan. The earlier you save for retirement, the more time you have to gain all the benefits of compound interest. If you open a retirement account at the age of 20 and consistently invest, your money will benefit from compound interest and build wealth at the age of 60.

By investing and reinvesting, you'll be able to build wealth and rely on the income you made during your frugal years, which allows you to fund your dreams. Frugal investors should learn about building wealth immediately and make saving and investing a habit for future financial success.

In order to invest wisely, you need to have an updated knowledge of available tools. You can either manage the whole cycle on your own by learning how to analyze, purchase and sell assets. You'll also want to monitor your investment portfolio from time to time to make sure that you have a wide range of investments that provide you with income no matter what the conditions are in the economy.

Another option would be to hire a professional financial advisor who can lead you to financial success. There are many investing options available, the important thing is to find one that matches your savings and investing goals. Check with your employer and contribute to a retirement plan, if available, such as 401(k) or 403(b). Take your time to learn about the different retirement plans available, see if your employer matches your contributions and what you can spend that money on to assist you in your other life goals such as buying a house or investing in the stock market.

Some employers also offer pension packages. Pension plans can influence your decision to pick one employer over another when you are making a choice of where to work. If your current job offers no retirement strategy, you can put your retirement savings in an Individual Retirement Account. You can also invest money in the stock market. This can be done in mutual funds and exchange-traded funds. With the Internet, it is easier than ever to make an automated investing plan that occurs on the same day every month. By automating your finances, you take the work out of saving and investing your money, and it comes naturally over time.

Apart from maintaining retirement accounts, there are many other investment alternatives that will provide you with a monthly income. One way to build assets is by purchasing property and renting it out. You can also buy shares in real estate investments and gain fixed profits over time. Investing in real estate requires a sufficient time for the investment to mature and active involvement but can lead to financial freedom.

Other options include purchasing gold and silver and selling it at a later date. There has been a significant rise in the price of gold over the last few years, however, it can be a risky option as the prices can also drop, depending on international market trends. You can also consider investing in small businesses owned by trustworthy acquaintances. If the business grows over time, you might end up enjoying profits. Make sure that you make investing decisions based on your goals and avoid speculative investments that are riskier and may not pay off in the end.

Remember that just because you stop working for an employer doesn't mean that you cannot do what you love! Retirement is a time where you can follow your passions, do the things that you've always wanted to do or work for yourself. Even after retirement, you should keep up your frugal lifestyle and be conscious of the lifestyle you lead. Start saving for retirement today by living a frugal lifestyle and using your income to build wealth for the future!

Chapter 10: Life Hacks to Help You Stay Frugal

Adopting a frugal lifestyle allows you to obtain financial stability and also provides freedom from debt and stress. Are you ready to apply some simple life hacks so that you can increase the amount of savings and investing you do and stretch your dollar even further? Let's discuss the top life hacks that are useful for saving time and money.

Life Hack #1: Save Money on Food

Food is a basic necessity that you can save money on by making a few basic changes. Cook food in bulk and plan out your meals throughout the week. Take home-cooked meals to work to save money that you might spend on dining out. You'll not only save money by not dining out, but you'll also reduce your transportation costs as well. Buy fresh or frozen fruits and vegetables instead of ones that come in a can. They not only contain preservative chemicals, which are detrimental for your health, but also cost two times more than fresh items that can be bought at wholesale rates. Purchase food while it's on sale in bulk and freeze what you can't use immediately. Make a rough plan of meals for the entire week or month and shop only for what's required to make those meals. Grow your own fresh produce in your backyard or in a community garden.

Life Hack #2: Save Money on Clothing

Clothing is another essential expense that is easy to splurge on and spend more than you have in your monthly budget. Make wise clothing choices and purchase items that are high quality. Purchase items off-season for the biggest savings. You can save 50% to 75% by buying clothes off-season, and even more if you purchase off-season at second hand stores. Secondly, avoid window shopping in branded stores. You can buy name brands from vintage stores and thrift stores at a fraction of the price.

Usually, such stores have huge discounts on great items just because of some unnoticeable tear or stain. You need to search carefully so that you don't end up buying something that will fall apart quickly. Shop online so that you can compare prices and look for the most competitive options. There are lots of clothing websites and even Facebook pages that sell unique designs and quality fabrics at low prices. Follow your favorite shopping brands to be notified of special deals and offers.

Purchase simple clothing that goes well with all other colors. Look for a deal offering clothing items in bulk. Often Internet retailers will promote pants, shirts, and undergarments in bulk for low prices so that you can save on the basics. With these simple life hacks, you can end up dressing great for a low cost.

Life Hack #3: Save Money on Household Items

There are some really simple ways to save money on household items that can result in hundreds of dollars' worth of savings each month. One effective way to save money is to end your cable subscription. It's really simple to cut the cord on cable with subscription services like Netflix and Hulu, as well as streaming players like Roku and Apple TV, which are a fraction of the price that you pay for live television.

You can further reduce your household expenses by removing your landline phone service if you have a mobile phone. Purchase a simple mobile phone that sends texts and makes calls but avoid an expensive data package. The latest smartphones not only come at a premium price, but they also have expensive monthly packages.

Some other things that reduce your monthly expenses are making sure that you switch off lights and other appliances when not in use. When you remember to unplug the electronics you aren't using, you can save 10% off of your electric bill, which adds up every month.

Reuse glass bottles and jars. They can be used later for storing spices, other foods and even be used as kitchen utensils. Use simple, natural household cleaners instead of expensive, chemical alternatives. Put vinegar in a spray bottle and use it as a liquid cleaner. Make smart purchases on household items by purchasing second hand or asking your friends and family if they have any furniture they're not using. Someone might be planning to renovate their house or sell their old furniture.

Move into a smaller house, which can be both comfortable and sufficient enough for you. You can save on maintenance costs along with paying a lower rental rate. Downsize wherever you can to cut down on expenses and look for alternatives to the items that you use daily.

Life Hack #4: Save on Travel Expenses

If you need to travel, analyze how you can save on fuel. Walk, bike or take public transit to save money and gain health benefits. If you cannot use these commuting methods, try to carpool with coworkers. Make sure to run errands at the same time instead of making multiple trips. Learn to manage with a single car instead of keeping a separate car for every family member.

Life Hack #5: Save on Entertainment Expenses

Have fun by finding cheaper ways to entertain yourself. Watch movies after they are released on DVD and avoid going to an overpriced, movie theater. Plan fun trips to parks and beaches with your family. Volunteer at events that you want to attend instead of buying tickets. Spend time at the library instead of purchasing books. These activities hardly cost you anything and give you the opportunity of spending quality time with your family.